STUDY GUIDE

The Promise Keeper

The God of the Covenants

R.C. Sproul

LIGONIER MINISTRIES
Renew your Mind.
LIGONIER.ORG | 800-435-4343

400 Technology Park Lake Mary, FL 32746
E-mail: info@ligonier.org

1

The Covenant of Redemption

MESSAGE INTRODUCTION

Knowing God means knowing that He is and will be utterly faithful to His covenant on our behalf. Scripture does not give us the full details of the plan that took place between the Triune Godhead in the past. But it does disclose the manifestation of that covenant in time—from God's redemptive work through the nation of Israel in the stories of the Old Testament to the culminating appearance of the God-Man, Jesus the Christ. In this lecture, Dr. R.C. Sproul explores the covenantal theme in Scripture and the foundational intra-Trinitarian covenant of redemption.

SCRIPTURE READINGS

Psalm 89:3-4; Isaiah 42:5-9; 53:10-12; Luke 22:28-30; John 10:18; 17:4-5

LEARNING OBJECTIVES

1. To understand the centrality of the covenantal theme in Scripture.
2. To be able to articulate what the covenant of redemption is, and how it relates to God's work of reconciling His creation to Himself.

QUOTATION

And Peter said to them, "Repent and be baptized every one of you in the name of Jesus Christ for the forgiveness of your sins, and you will receive the gift of the Holy Spirit. For the promise is for you and for your children and for all who are far off, everyone whom the Lord our God calls to himself."

—Acts 2:38-39

LECTURE OUTLINE

I. Scriptural Theme: Covenant
   a. The whole concept of "covenant" is basic to understanding Scripture. We can go so far as to say that God's work with and in creation is couched in covenantal terms.
   b. One major principle of this Scriptural theme is that revelation is progressive. That is, each subsequent revelation from God is not a corrective on what He has previously said; rather, each revelation augments or adds content to the previous one.
   c. The word covenant does not simply mean "agreement." We must not allow our own western conceptions of "covenant" to dictate the Scriptural meaning. But many of our own conceptions do have elements found in the biblical covenants (e.g., "promises").
   d. Biblical covenants have a more profound religiosity inherent in them. They are wrought by divine sanction, and depict an integral relationship between promises and fulfillments (i.e., God *always* fulfills His word.).
   e. Thus, the Christian is to walk by faith—a faith that is nothing less than being fully persuaded of the promises of God, which will lead us in gratitude to live in covenant with Him.
   f. This, of course, is impossible to do without His grace. While we have not seen or heard God, His Word has been given for this reason: to attest to His covenant faithfulness.

II. The Covenant of Redemption
   a. Much controversy surrounded Jesus during His lifetime. From whence did He come? By whose authority? What was His origin? The answers to these questions bear on this first covenant among the Godhead.
   b. Christ Jesus did not come to change what God had revealed prior to His arrival, or as is commonly misunderstood, to show mercy in contradistinction to the Old Testament "God of wrath."
   c. All along, Jesus was doing the will of His Father. They were one in their eternal purpose. He did nothing on His own initiative, but came because of an intra-Trinitarian covenant—a covenant that was not "Plan B."
   d. In this covenant, the Father sent the Son, the Son accomplished the plan, and the Spirit applied the Son's accomplished work to the people of the Triune God.
   e. Typically, Jesus' work in redemption is discussed in two ways:
   f. *Perfect Active Obedience:* Jesus actively and willfully put Himself under the Law of God (e.g., He was baptized just as sinners in need of cleansing were to do). Jesus needed to accomplish all that God required Israel to do. Thus, He became the embodiment of Israel. And as the Israel of God, He achieved perfect righteousness and earned redemption for His people.

g. *Perfect Passive Obedience:* This work Jesus did on the cross. He subjugated Himself to the curses of the covenant, to the judgment and wrath of the Father, on behalf of His people.

STUDY QUESTIONS

1. Each subsequent covenant revealed in Scripture corrects the problems with God's previous plan.
   a. True
   b. False
   c. Both true and false
   d. I don't know

2. The covenant of redemption describes ___________.
   a. The intra-Trinitarian agreement to redeem a people for God's glory
   b. The intra-Trinitarian agreement to damn a people for God's glory
   c. Both a and b
   d. None of the above

3. The covenant of redemption was God's ___________.
   a. Response to what had taken Him by surprise: the Fall of man
   b. Response to the Israelite nation's failure to keep the covenant of works
   c. Plan to provide salvation for sinners via the death of Jesus on the cross
   d. None of the above

4. Which of the following best describes the "active obedience" of Jesus?
   a. The passion (death and resurrection)
   b. Jesus put Himself under the Law of God and perfectly abided in it.
   c. Jesus put Himself under the Law of God and abolished all of it.
   d. All of the above

5. Much of the Bible is couched in ___________ terms.
   a. Scientific
   b. Covenantal
   c. Both a and b
   d. None of the above

6. By whose authority did Jesus come to earth?
   a. His own
   b. The Father's
   c. The Holy Spirit's
   d. All of the above

BIBLE STUDY AND DISCUSSION QUESTIONS

1. Explain how the covenant of redemption relates to the salvation of sinners in time.

2. Are there any portions of Scripture that come to mind when discussing God's definite plan for his work of redemption?

3. Is the covenant of redemption inconsistent with the idea that we have the free will to choose according to our desires? Explain your answer.

4. In the covenant of redemption, did the Father agree to call out classes (i.e., a certain group of people) or individuals into the service of the Son?

5. Can you define or describe any faulty views that you may have heard or read on this subject? How would you respond to the person who argues that the idea of this covenant is pure speculation?

6. In what sense is Jesus the Son subordinate to God the Father?

7. What portions of Scripture show that Jesus voluntarily took His task upon Himself (for starters, John 10:18, Phil. 2:8)?

SUGGESTED READING FOR FURTHER STUDY

Robertson, O. Palmer. *The Christ of the Covenants,* pp. 3-25, 91-2

2

The Meaning of "Covenant"

MESSAGE INTRODUCTION

The word *covenant* gets tossed around a lot—especially in Reformed circles. The difficulty lies in the fact that "covenant" remains a hard concept to comprehend. Yet it is treated by many theologians as a central interpretive principle of Scripture and Israel's history. Is it really all that important? Do we really miss something in Scripture if we leave the study of biblical covenants up to the scholars? The answer is a resounding "Yes!" In this lecture, Dr. R.C. Sproul expounds on the meaning of "covenant" and its development in the early history of translation.

SCRIPTURE READINGS

Genesis 21:27; 26:28; 31:44; Judges 2:1-2; Ezra 10:3; Proverbs 2:16-17; Ezekiel 16:8; Malachi 2:14

LEARNING OBJECTIVE

To understand the meaning of the word covenant as it relates to God's covenant with man.

QUOTATION

Know therefore that the Lord your God is God, the faithful God who keeps covenant and steadfast love with those who love him and keep his commandments, to a thousand generations....

—Deuteronomy 7:9

LECTURE OUTLINE

I. Biblical words
   a. *Berit*: This Hebrew word is translated in English "covenant." When used to describe God's covenant with man, it simply refers to an agreement that rests on God's sovereignty with divine sanction.
   b. *Diatheke*: The scholars who translated the Old Testament into Greek (c. 250 BC) used this Greek word meaning "testament" for the Hebrew word *berit*. While not an equivalent meaning, "testament" does denote the notion that God sovereignly covenants with whomever He wills.
      - This translation has led to some confusion. A "testament" can be changed any time by the testator. He or she can disinherit those previously in the testament. But God's testament is steadfast.
      - Another inadequacy of this word *testament* comes from the fact that the benefits of a testament come *after* the death of the testator—not before.
   c. *Suntheke:* This Greek word was rejected because it denoted more of a mutual commitment, purpose, origin, and obligation. The Bible depicts God as the One who is utterly faithful to the covenant, needing to rely on no one for its completion.
   d. We must keep in mind that the "Testaments" of the Old and New are literary divisions, and we must not confuse that use of "testament" with the biblical concept of "covenant." Who was the greatest prophet of the Old Testament? Is his story found within the pages of the Old Testament?
   e. Our story about the old covenant begins with the fall of man. But was there any "arrangement" between God and Adam before he fell? The next three lectures will explore this aspect of biblical covenants.

STUDY QUESTIONS

1. "Berit" is the Hebrew word for "____________" in English.
   a. Thanksgiving
   b. Faithfulness
   c. Covenant
   d. None of the above

2. What English word is translated from the Greek work *diatheke?*
   a. Mutual commitment
   b. Mutual purpose
   c. Testament
   d. None of the above

3. God is depicted in Scripture as one who is utterly faithful to the covenant, ___________.
    a. Yet needing to rely on a person's sanction to enact the covenant
    b. Needing to rely on no one for its completion
    c. Needing only to start it, while relying on us to finish it
    d. None of the above

4. Who was the greatest prophet of the Old Testament?
    a. Isaiah
    b. John the Baptist
    c. Jeremiah
    d. None of the above

5. The "Old Testament" refers to ___________.
    a. The Mosaic covenant
    b. The Abrahamic covenant
    c. The Davidic covenant
    d. The compilation of ancient writings from Genesis to Malachi

6. Our story about the old covenant begins with ___________.
    a. The covenant of redemption
    b. The rise of David to the throne
    c. Noah's flood
    d. The fall of man

BIBLE STUDY AND DISCUSSION QUESTIONS

1. Was the relationship Adam enjoyed in the Garden with God necessary due to Adam's being created? Or was it a gracious privilege? What parameters did God choose to define that relationship ("berit," "diatheke")?

2. Why are the various arrangements God has made with humanity properly called "covenants"?

3. What are some of the elements of a biblical covenant as described in this lecture?

4. Do you think that the Bible itself warrants reading it in a covenantal framework, or do you think this has been wrongfully superimposed upon the Scriptures? Defend your answer biblically.

5. According to this lecture and the previous lecture, what are the roles of the Father, Son, and the Holy Spirit in the covenant of redemption? Are there any Scripture passages that inform your answer?

6. Read John 17: 18-19 and Galatians 4:4. How do these contribute to our understanding of an agreement between the Godhead before Creation?

7. Define the words *berit* and *diatheke,*and how the latter is more appropriate than *suntheke* when describing the covenant between God and man.

SUGGESTED READING FOR FURTHER STUDY

Robertson, O. Palmer. *The Christ of the Covenants,* pp. 27-53
Vos, Geerhardus. *Biblical Theology: Old and New Testaments,* pp. 19-26

3

Creation Covenant, Part 1

MESSAGE INTRODUCTION

The first covenant made between God and humanity took place in the Garden of Eden. It has been called many things, and there are as many opinions about it as there are theologians. But essential to our understanding of this first covenant is how it relates to the gracious covenant which was to follow. Some scholars contend that there just is no Scriptural warrant for calling this agreement in the garden a "covenant." Dr. R.C. Sproul contends otherwise, for a basic understanding of this as covenant is necessary if we are to understand the finished work of the living Savior. In this lecture, Dr. Sproul will discuss and explain the various names given this covenant.

SCRIPTURE READING

Genesis 2:17; Romans 5:12-20; 10:5; Galatians 3:10-14

LEARNING OBJECTIVE

To recognize and understand the various names for God's covenant with man in the Garden of Eden.

QUOTATIONS

So God created man in his own image, in the image of God he created him; male and female he created them.

And God blessed them. And God said to them, "Be fruitful and multiply and fill the earth and subdue it and have dominion over the fish of the sea and over the birds of the heavens and over every living thing that moves on the earth."

—Genesis 1:27-28

The first covenant made with man was a covenant of works, wherein life was promised to Adam, and in him to his posterity, upon condition of perfect and personal obedience.
—The Westminster Confession of Faith, 7.2

LECTURE OUTLINE

I. The First Covenant with Man
   a. This covenant is known by various names for different reasons.
   b. *Adamic Covenant*: The word *Adam* actually means "humanity." God made a covenant not just with the historic person, Adam, but with those whom he represented. This concept is most succinctly articulated in Saint Paul's letter to the Romans, wherein the author makes much ado about the "first" and "second" Adam.
      - They both worked as representatives of the entire human race. This means that those who descended from Adam are by necessity in a covenant relationship with God. It cannot be escaped or denied. Ethnicity makes no difference whatsoever. Thus, the big question is this: Are we covenant-breakers or covenant-keepers? All of humanity falls into one camp or the other.
   c. *Creation Covenant*: called thus because covenantal-type sanctions were imposed upon the entire created order. None of these have ever been abrogated. Any divine sanction put into effect at creation extends as far as creation itself. One example of this would be the sanctity of marriage. We recognize marriage in the civilized world because marriage is for *all* humanity—not just for the ancient Israelites or Christians.
      i. If rooted or grounded in the act of creation, a law cannot be reduced to cultural custom.
      ii. In order to best understand certain portions of Scripture, we need to grasp the difference between "customs" and "principles."
      - Customs change, but the over-arching principles do not. For example, with respect to the way we dress: do ladies wear hats or not? Must we evangelize without shoes on like Jesus instructed His disciples to do? Is male headship in the home custom or principle?
   d. *Covenant of Works:* This third common name for the first covenant God made with man is by far the most controversial. Why? Because many see it as an intrusion of systematic theology onto biblical theology. But the critic should remember that any time the Bible's main themes are being summarized that systematic theology is taking place. Both approaches to theology have proved equally helpful to the Church.
      i. In Reformed theology in general, and the Westminster Confession of Faith in particular, a distinction is made between the covenant of works and the covenant of grace:
      - Any benefit the creature gets comes by God's own personal disposition. The creature is not entitled to anything, God owes us nothing,

but he gives voluntarily (see WCF 7.1). We therefore owe him everything, that is, we owe him our very existence.

- God, in the sheer act of communicating with his creatures, must condescend to them. This condescension God accommodates to our human understanding, and therefore takes the shape of a covenant.

ii. Our next lecture will cover the distinctions between the covenant of works and the covenant of grace.

STUDY QUESTIONS

1. Which of the following is *not* a name for the covenant between Adam and his Creator?
   a. The Adamic covenant
   b. The covenant of works
   c. The covenant of redemption
   d. The Creation covenant

2. The word adam actually means "____________"
   a. Male
   b. Humanity
   c. Clay
   d. One

3. The first covenant God made with man is often called "the Adamic covenant" because ____________.
   a. That was the first man's name, "Adam"
   b. The covenant was made with Adam and the entire race he represented
   c. Adam took the initiative in making this covenant with God
   d. None of the above

4. The first covenant God made outside of Himself is often called "the Creation covenant" because ____________.
   a. It was made with the first man
   b. Covenantal-type sanctions were imposed only upon the animal kingdom
   c. God "created" a covenant with Adam and Eve
   d. Covenantal-type sanctions were imposed upon the entire created order

5. The main difference between customs and principles is that ____________.
   a. There is no difference
   b. Customs change, but the over-arching principles do not
   c. Principles change, but the over-arching customs do not
   d. None of the above

6. The covenant of works—by far the most controversial name for the first covenant God made with man is ___________.
    a. Not to be distinguished from the covenant of grace
    b. A result of systematizing biblical theology
    c. Both a and b
    d. None of the above

BIBLE STUDY AND DISCUSSION QUESTIONS

1. Read Romans 5:12-21. What might be the biblical reasons for calling the covenant between God and Adam "Adamic"?

2. How does a clear understanding of the Adamic covenant help us follow the gist of Saint Paul's argument in 1 Corinthians 15:12-28?

3. Read Genesis 1-2. What parts of this passage accentuate elements emphasized in the "Creation covenant"?

4. Using Scripture, describe some of the covenantal-type sanctions that God imposed upon His created order.

5. What are your opinions about customs and principles, and how do they relate to the issues discussed in this lecture?

6. Explain why the covenant of works must be considered a gracious condescension on the part of God?

7. Are any of the various names for this covenant better than the others? Why or why not? Do you think systematic theology imposes unbiblical principles upon the sacred text?

SUGGESTED READING FOR FURTHER STUDY

Robertson, O. Palmer. *The Christ of the Covenants*, pp. 67-74

4

Creation Covenant, Part 2

MESSAGE INTRODUCTION

Continuing our study of the Creation covenant, we turn our attention to the elements of the probationary period established in the garden. Central to this probation were the two trees. What did they symbolize? How are they to be understood? Was the act of eating fruit really all that bad? In this lecture, Dr. R.C. Sproul explains the different aspects of the covenant of works, and begins his discussion on the two trees and their relationship to this period in biblical history.

SCRIPTURE READINGS

Genesis 2:15-17; Leviticus 18:5; Deuteronomy 27:26; Nehemiah 9:29; Matthew 19:16-17; James 2:10

LEARNING OBJECTIVES

1. To understand the distinctions between the covenants of works and grace.
2. To be able to recognize what elements of the Garden of Eden narrative have led theologians to discuss it in covenantal terms.

QUOTATION

The Lord God took the man and put him in the garden of Eden to work it and keep it. And the Lord God commanded the man, saying "You may surely eat of every tree of the garden, but of the tree of the knowledge of good and evil you shall not eat, for in the day that you eat of it you shall surely die."

—Genesis 2:15-17

> *Therefore, as one trespass led to condemnation for all men, so one act of righteousness leads to justification and life for all men. For as by the one man's disobedience the many were made sinners, so by the one man's obedience the many will be made righteous... Thus it is written, "The first man Adam became a living being"; the last Adam became a life-giving spirit.*
>
> —Romans 5:18-19; 1 Corinthians 15:45

LECTURE OUTLINE

I. Elements of the covenant of works:
   a. On the condition of man's obedience to the sanctions of this covenant, God would confer the blessings of the covenant (life eternal in His presence).
   b. But since man failed, God established a covenant of grace that fulfilled the covenant of works without relying on the obedience of fallen humanity.
   c. This discussion drives us to understand the nature of mankind in the Garden of Eden. The best way to approach this question is by looking at how the post-fall image of God in man has been shattered (though not utterly destroyed).
   d. Bishop Augustine of Hippo wrote that Adam and Eve were endowed with a gift that, if lost, was not essential to their humanity. That is, it did not make them "less than human" when they lost it.
   e. Furthermore, in order for Adam to fulfill the covenant of works he needed two things: 1) Innocence: Humanity was created good, but not without the potential to do bad. 2) Positive Righteousness: This righteousness, or "utter faithfulness," requires *active* obedience. This perfect obedience would thus entail earning the blessing of the covenant.
   f. Adam and Eve, however, were number one (innocent), but not number two above (positively righteous), as they were positively unrighteous in their failure of the covenant. It is because of Christ Jesus' positive righteousness that all who believe in Him regain Paradise. But once we believe in Him, if we are then put back under the covenant of works, we would utterly fail again. So, what do we Christians actually regain?
   g. Since man was in a probationary period in the garden (e.g., "If you eat of the Tree of the Knowledge of Good and Evil, then you shall surely die."), Jesus came to do what Adam failed to do, that is, obey perfectly God's commands. Thus in His perfect and positive righteousness, Jesus won or earned the rewards of the covenant and then passes them on to all who would believe in Him.

II. The Two Trees
   a. The Tree of Life: The life inherent in this tree's fruit represents the highest possible potency of life (cf. John 10:10b). In the new heavens and new earth, the life conferred to those who believe in the Christ will be a higher life than the one given to Adam and Eve in the garden.

b. It will be greater because believers will be made immutably righteous, that is, they will be unable to sin. Adam and Eve were not given this attribute, as they were merely able not to sin. Only a victorious Adam could dispense with such a blessing, giving to those who overcome "the tree of life, which is in the paradise of God" (Rev. 2:7).
c. The Tree of the Knowledge of Good and Evil: The knowledge of this tree represents a knowledge that Adam and Eve were not meant to have until God's good timing.
d. God tells them not to eat of this tree, for if they do, they will die immediately. This condition represents the period of probation or testing about which the covenant of works speaks. While God does not tempt (i.e., entice to sin) Adam and Eve, He does test them.
e. In like manner, Jesus was also put to the test (Mark 1:12-13). The temptation narrative parallels the temptation of Adam, but the second Adam accomplished what Adam the First failed to do.

STUDY QUESTIONS

1. What was the condition that had to be met by Adam in order for God to confer the blessings of the covenant upon him?
   a. Adam had to name every animal in the garden.
   b. Adam had to obey God's word to not eat of a certain tree.
   c. Adam had to attain divinity by obtaining god-like knowledge.
   d. None of the above

2. The image of God in humankind had been ____________ as a result of the Fall.
   a. Utterly destroyed
   b. Shattered
   c. Unaffected
   d. None of the above

3. Adam's "innocence" refers to his ____________ .
   a. Inability to sin
   b. Inability to not sin
   c. Ability to sin
   d. None of the above

4. "Positive Righteousness" is ____________ .
   a. Becoming like God by obtaining complete knowledge
   b. Doing one's best, which would fulfill the covenant
   c. Perfect, active obedience to God's word, which would fulfill the covenant
   d. Both a and b

5. On the final day, believers will be ___________ .
   a. Able to sin
   b. Unable to not sin
   c. Unable to sin
   d. None of the above

6. What did God say would happen to Adam and Eve if they ate from the tree of the knowledge of good and evil?
   a. "You shall know all things, good and evil."
   b. "You shall not surely die!"
   c. "You shall surely die."
   d. None of the above

BIBLE STUDY AND DISCUSSION QUESTIONS

1. Define and describe the several elements of the covenant of works. Use Scripture to support your answer.

2. What was the promise of the covenant of works? What Scripture passages support your answer?

3. Upon what condition was the covenant of works resting? What was the penalty for failing this covenant? Cite those portions of Scripture that support this understanding of the covenant.

4. Why is it so import to Christian theology that Adam and Eve be representatives of the entire human race?

5. According to this lecture (see A.5 above), Adam was created innocent, though able to sin. Do we share this in common with him? Why or why not? Support your answer from Scripture.

6. Have you heard anyone argue that we are born morally innocent? How would you respond? How might this notion undermine the work of Christ?

7. In your own words, explain how this agreement in the Garden between God and Adam is best defined in covenantal terms. If you do not agree that it is best defined in covenantal terms, then explain why it does not and how we might better define it.

SUGGESTED READING FOR FURTHER STUDY

Robertson, O. Palmer. *The Christ of the Covenants*, pp. 74-87
Vos, Geerhardus. *Biblical Theology: Old and New Testaments*, pp. 27-40

5

Creation Covenant, Part 3

MESSAGE INTRODUCTION

In this final lecture on the covenant of works, the tree of knowledge of good and evil is discussed in detail. The tree itself stood as the ultimate test for Adam and Eve: Were they simply going to trust God and His wisdom, or would they reach out in a godless grasp toward that which was not theirs? In this lecture, Dr. R.C. Sproul discusses the forbidden tree and the curse of the Fall.

SCRIPTURE READING

Genesis 2:15-17; Hosea 6:1-10; Matthew 5:19; Galatians 3:10; James 2:10

LEARNING OBJECTIVES

1. To understand more fully what the tree of the knowledge of good and evil symbolized.
2. To understand the elements of the curse after humanity had fallen.

QUOTATION

For I desire steadfast love and not sacrifice, the knowledge of God rather than burnt offerings. But like Adam they transgressed the covenant; there they dealt faithlessly with me.

—Hosea 6:6-7

LECTURE OUTLINE

I. The Tree of the Knowledge of Good and Evil
    a. Typically, the explanation offered for the name of this tree is that Adam and Eve had no experiential knowledge of good and evil, and upon eating the tree (and thus sinning), they would gain that knowledge.

b. However, Adam and Eve were created as moral agents with the ability to discern between good and evil (e.g., obeying God = good; disobeying God = evil). The serpent's temptation sheds more light on this subject.
c. The tempter basically argued that our first parents only thought they were free. True freedom, the serpent quipped, is autonomous (a law unto oneself). Humankind, however, was created free but not autonomous. There are restrictions to our freedom, namely, that we are to be dependent upon our Creator, who is the only one who knows good and evil perfectly.
d. The serpent challenges this notion by arguing that limited freedom is not freedom at all. He directly contradicted God's word by saying that Adam and Eve will not die when they eat of the tree. The only reason they were forbidden, according to the serpent, was that God wanted to hold them back from reaching their fullest potential—doing what is right in one's own eyes.
e. Thus, the tree represented a knowledge that Adam and Eve were not meant to have until God's timing. And the heinous sin of the Fall was the human grasp for autonomous freedom—taking from the tree regardless of God's word and independent of His guidance. This is what broke the covenant of creation.
f. Punishment for breaking the covenant was supposed to bring immediate death. Adam and Eve did suffer spiritual death that day, but God graciously stayed His hand from killing them physically. He instead killed an animal for its skin, so the two humans could be covered (this prefigured the Messiah's covering His people with His righteousness). The biblical story from Genesis 3 onward is the story of God's work of redemption.

II. The Curse
a. The first thing to recognize about this curse is that it carried with it its antithesis: blessing.
b. Man: While already a tiller of the garden, the ground would now yield reluctantly.
c. Woman: The woman's pain in giving birth would now be greatly increased.
d. Serpent: The curse against the serpent was that it would crawl on its belly. It also received the damning oracle that a seed from the woman will crush the serpent's head—not without damage to his heel. The irony here is that the very first proclamation of the Gospel comes amidst the curse of the Fall.
e. God's first redemptive act occurs when Adam and Eve, ashamed of their nakedness, are covered with animal skins through the shedding of blood. This foreshadows the righteous garments of Christ that cover our nakedness—garments that also came through the shedding of blood.

STUDY QUESTIONS

1. Did Adam and Eve know what was evil before they ate of the forbidden tree?
    a. Yes
    b. No
    c. Maybe
    d. I don't know

2. True freedom, according to the serpent, ___________ .
    a. Is impossible
    b. Is autonomous
    c. Is trusting in God's word
    d. None of the above

3. Adam and Eve were to be dependent on ___________ for their knowledge of good and evil.
    a. Each other
    b. The serpent
    c. Adam
    d. God

4. The breaking of the covenant involved ___________ .
    a. Eating of the forbidden tree
    b. The grasp for autonomous freedom
    c. God's forcing Adam and Eve to disobey Him
    d. Both a and b

5. Even amidst the curse of the Fall, we can see ___________ .
    a. God's fear of man
    b. A promised blessing
    c. Both a and b
    d. None of the above

6. God's first redemptive act occurs ___________ .
    a. At the cross on Calvary
    b. When Noah is saved from the flood
    c. When Adam and Eve are covered with animal skins
    d. Before the foundation of the world

BIBLE STUDY AND DISCUSSION QUESTIONS

1. In your own words, explain what the tree of the knowledge of good and evil represented, and how the serpent twisted it to serve his argument.

2. After reading the biblical account of the Fall (Gen. 3), how would you explain the nature of the sin committed by Adam and Eve (eating an apple can't be all that bad, can it)? What do you think their motives were in sinning?

3. When we speak of the origin of sin, on whom can the blame be laid? How do we reconcile this and that fact that God is sovereign over all events?

4. Explain the various elements of the curse of the Fall, as well as the blessings implied therein. How was the moral and spiritual character of Adam and Eve affected after their fall into sin?

5. Why are we also guilty of Adam's first sin? Use Scripture to support your answer.

6. Using Scripture, show that the doctrine of depravity is clearly taught by its authors. Include in you answer what the Scriptures teach regarding how the image of God in man was affected and the time when we who are in Adam actually become depraved (in the womb or as children?).

7. How does God's "first redemptive act" prefigure the work of Christ?

SUGGESTED READING FOR FURTHER STUDY

Robertson, O. Palmer. *The Christ of the Covenants*, pp. 93-107
Vos, Geerhardus. *Biblical Theology: Old and New Testaments*, pp. 41-44

6

Noahic Covenant

MESSAGE INTRODUCTION

In the evil generation preceding the time of the great flood, only Noah walked with God. He stood in stark contrast to those whose actions and thoughts were continually evil. Finally, God had had enough. The sins of the earth were full, and it was time to start again. Making a covenant with Noah and his family, God chose to graciously save them from the perilous deep. In so doing, God subdued once again the chaotic waters and put his chosen one, Noah, in charge as the steward of creation. In this lecture, Dr. R.C. Sproul explains the Noahic covenant and its relationship to the overarching covenantal theme in Scripture.

SCRIPTURE READING

Genesis 8:20-9:27

LEARNING OBJECTIVE

To be able to summarize the most important elements of the Noahic covenant, and how they relate to Scripture as a whole.

QUOTATIONS

And God blessed Noah and his sons and said to them, "Be fruitful and multiply and fill the earth....I give you everything....Behold, I establish my covenant with you and your offspring after you, and with every living creature that is with you...that never again shall all flesh be cut off by the waters of the flood, and never again shall there be a flood to destroy the earth." And God said, "This is the sign of the covenant that I make between me and you and every living creature that is with you, for all future generations: I have set my bow in the cloud, and it shall be sign of the covenant between me and the earth."

—Genesis 9:1, 3, 9-13

LECTURE OUTLINE

I. The Noahic Covenant
   a. We have already looked at the distinction between the covenants of grace and works, and have seen that every covenant after the Fall is to be looked at under the heading of the covenant of grace.
   b. The first covenant we come to in the biblical story after the creation covenant is broken is the covenant God made with Noah.
   c. The social background building up to this covenant is described in the Bible as a wicked time (Gen. 6:1-8). There was a radical expansion of evil in the world that began most notably with the murder of Abel (4:1-12). The lines of Seth and Cain are then juxtaposed.
   d. At the time of Genesis 6, wickedness spread exponentially as the "sons of God" took wives in an ungodly manner. All of the world is filled with evil, "but Noah found favor in the eyes of the Lord" (v.8).
   e. In Genesis 6:3, God declares that His spirit shall not abide in man forever. That is, He will allow men to rebel until their sin has reached its fullness. The 120 years is probably the span of time between this proclamation and the Flood, at which time God judged the people for their utter wickedness.
   f. We must see that it is God who graciously restrains us from being utterly depraved (distinct from totally depraved). Once God removes His restraining hand, the door is open to unspeakable sin.
   g. In Genesis 6:8, we see that God's favor was upon Noah. "Grace" is the definitive word in God's relationship with Noah. In verse 9 we see that Noah was "blameless," which means "complete"—not "sinless." When someone is said to "walk with God" or is described as "obedient to God," the highest compliments have been paid to that person.

II. Life after the flood (Gen. 8:20ff.):
   a. God ratifies His covenant with Noah through sacrifice. The terms involve making promises (on God's part).
   b. We gain another glimpse of God's redemption at this point. The beneficiaries of the covenant of grace are not only God's people, but the entire earth (Gen. 8:22-23; 9:9-10). This is why Saint Paul describes Christ Jesus as the cosmic Christ, the one who brings *all* of creation into reconciliation to Him.
   c. Notice that in many respects, the Noahic covenant recapitulates elements from the creation mandate ("Be fruitful and multiply...I give you everything" [plants and animals]; Gen. 9:1,3).
   d. Is Genesis 9:6 a mere truism that violent people meet violent deaths? In all probability it is more than that. It is the covenantal institution of capital punishment. Because this covenant is global in scope, so, too, is this mandate to be carried out globally.

e. God's people sanction capital punishment for the very same reason they abhor abortion—the sanctity of life. This punishment was given to preserve human life. Wanton killing is an attack on the life-giver Himself. Thus, the person forfeits his life.
f. The sign of the Noahic covenant: the Rainbow. The terms of this promise cover the whole earth. It is perpetual, and the promise to preserve creation shall be kept by God's own word—which creation, by the way, is the realm in which His redemptive plan is enacted.

STUDY QUESTIONS

1. Every covenant after the fall can probably be categorized under the ___________.
   a. Covenant of works
   b. Covenant of grace
   c. The Noahic covenant
   d. None of the above

2. The time building up to Noah's flood was ___________.
   a. Filled with righteousness
   b. Marked by the world's passion for serving God
   c. Wicked and continually evil
   d. Partially corrupt and partially righteous

3. Without God's restraining grace we would be ___________.
   a. Partially depraved
   b. Totally depraved
   c. Utterly depraved
   d. Perfect

4. Noah's "blamelessness" meant that he was ___________.
   a. Worthy of God's covenant
   b. Sinless
   c. Unchallenged in his devotion to God and His commandments
   d. None of the above

5. The covenant of grace ___________.
   a. Benefits only those whom the Father had given to the Son
   b. Benefits the entire world
   c. Should not be distinguished from the covenant of redemption
   d. Should not be distinguished from the covenant of works

6. The sign of the Noahic covenant was ___________.
   a. Circumcision
   b. A raven
   c. A dove
   d. A rainbow

BIBLE STUDY AND DISCUSSION QUESTIONS

1. Read 1 Corinthians 10:9-12. Given that the Old Testament stories were written down for our instruction, what might we glean from the Noahic flood story that teaches us how to avoid evil? What does it teach about how God worked in the world during that time?

2. What do you think was the main purpose of this period of biblical history in its relation to God's overall plan of redemption? To get at this answer, describe the development of the human race before the flood, as well as God's restraining grace upon humanity (cf. Gen. 6:3). Why did God allow sin to march proudly through this age?

3. What state would the world be left in if God were to remove His grace completely? Use Scripture to support your answer.

4. Using Scripture, show that man is totally depraved as opposed to utterly depraved.

5. How was God's purpose in redemption furthered by saving Noah and his family? What child of Noah's will be the carrier of God's work of redemption?

6. Was the arrangement God made after the flood only with man? If not, what else was it made with? What was the sign of this covenant? How does this covenantal sign relate to that with which the covenant was made?

7. Describe the major elements of the Noahic covenant (cf. Gen. 8:20-9:17). Looking at Genesis 8:20, 15:9-10, 17:10-11, and Exodus 24:508, what common practice or element always accompanied the ratification of a covenant? Explain why.

SUGGESTED READING FOR FURTHER STUDY

Robertson, O. Palmer. *The Christ of the Covenants*, pp. 109-125
Vos, Geerhardus. *Biblical Theology: Old and New Testaments*, pp. 45-55

7

Abrahamic Covenant, Part 1

MESSAGE INTRODUCTION

The covenant made with the patriarch Abraham continues to see its fulfillment to this day. With each sinner's passage into so great a salvation, father Abraham's nation grows. The true Israel—made up of Jews *and* Gentiles—is indeed more numerous than the stars in heaven and the sands upon the shore. In this lecture, Dr. R.C. Sproul begins to explain the most important features of the Abrahamic covenant, and proves God's utter faithfulness to it.

SCRIPTURE READING

Genesis 15

LEARNING OBJECTIVE

To be able to articulate the background of the Abrahamic covenant.

QUOTATIONS

"Look toward heaven, and number the stars, if you are able to number them." Then [the Lord] said to him, "So shall your offspring be." And [Abram] believed the Lord, and he counted it to him as righteousness....When the sun had gone down and it was dark, behold, a smoking fire pot and a flaming torch passed between these pieces. On that day the Lord made a covenant with Abram, saying, "To your offspring I give this land..." [the land of Canaan].

—Genesis 15:5-6, 17-18

LECTURE OUTLINE

I. The Abrahamic covenant

a. In redemptive history, the patriarch Abraham emerged as "the father of the faithful." Mary herself made mention of him: "He has helped his servant Israel, in remembrance of his mercy, as he spoke to our fathers, to Abraham and to his offspring forever" (Luke 1:54-55). Saint Paul also uses Abraham as the preeminent example of justification by faith (Rom. 4).

b. In Genesis 12: 1-4, God called out a pagan among pagans, and Abraham responded in faith. Elements of the covenant include: 1) Abraham's offspring will be made into a great nation; 2) His name will be great; 3) People will be blessed or cursed depending on their relationship to him; and 4) All the nations and families of the earth will be blessed through Abraham's blessing.

c. The pattern of the promise is as follows: The promise is given to one (Abraham), and blesses the many (ethnic Israel); it then comes back to one (the Christ), and then goes back to the many (the true Israel-Jews and Gentiles).

d. At the beginning of Genesis 15, we see Abraham ask the Lord about the heir that was promised to him. It stems from Abraham's faith in the promise, but the problem was that Abraham had grown old.

e. Why did God wait? Was Abraham under judgment? Maybe God wanted to clearly manifest that the benefits of His covenant relied completely on His grace. That is, it gave God the opportunity to glorify His holy name.

f. Genesis 15:6: "And [Abraham] believed the Lord, and he counted it to him as righteousness." This text was Saint Paul's main proof from the Old Testament that justification was always by faith and not works. The apostle contended that the just shall live by faith. In this way, Christ Jesus' righteousness was imputed to those before His death in the same manner as it is even unto to this very day.

g. Abraham, in faith, still wonders how he can be certain that he will inherit the land (v.8).

h. Genesis 15:17 serves as the answer to Abraham's search for assurance: "When the sun had gone down and it was dark, behold, a smoking fire pot and a flaming torch passed between these pieces."

i. God Himself passed through the gauntlet alone, signifying that He alone is subject to the covenant curses if He does not follow through with the promises of the covenant. In our next lecture, we shall explore more deeply this dramatic event in redemptive history.

STUDY QUESTIONS

1. The preeminent example of a faithful man in the letter to the Romans is ___________.
    a. Adam
    b. Abel
    c. Abraham
    d. None of the above

2. Which patriarch emerged as the one most closely associated with redemptive history?
    a. Jacob
    b. Noah
    c. David
    d. None of the above

3. Which of the following is not an element of the Abrahamic covenant?
    a. Abraham's name will be great
    b. Abraham's offspring will be made into a great nation
    c. All the nations of the earth will be cursed through him
    d. All of the above

4. Which of the following is an element of the Abrahamic covenant?
    a. Nations will be blessed or cursed depending on their relationship to Abraham
    b. All the nations and families of the earth will be blessed through Abraham's blessing
    c. All of Abraham's offspring will be included in the kingdom of God
    d. Both a and b

5. In the letter to the Romans, Saint Paul cites which text from the Old Testament as proof that justification is by faith alone?
    a. Genesis 15:2
    b. Genesis 15:17
    c. Genesis 15:6
    d. Genesis 16:3

6. Abraham's thirst for assurance came from his ___________.
    a. Unbelief in God's promises
    b. Faith in God's promises
    c. Uncertainty in God's ability to give him a son
    d. None of the above

BIBLE STUDY AND DISCUSSION QUESTIONS

1. Read Genesis 12:1-9. What promises did God make to Abraham?

2. After reading Genesis 15, describe in your own words the events therein. How does this advance God's work of redemption in the world?

3. Read Jeremiah 34:18-19. How does it relate to the ceremony described in Genesis 15? What does it say regarding the penalty that would fall upon the one who broke the covenant?

4. Why is Genesis 15:6 so significant for us today (i.e., those of us in the new covenant)?

5. Read Genesis 18:17-19. What was God's purpose in choosing Abraham? How does this serve to advance His work of redemption?

6. How did Abraham's faith relate to the promises of God (did Abraham actually see any of the promises actualized?)? Why did God tarry so long before fulfilling those promises? Did it benefit Abraham? What might it have taught him?

7. Is there any room in this narrative to suggest that Abraham may have believed in or served many gods? From Scripture, point out that Abraham's faith was monotheistic.

SUGGESTED READING FOR FURTHER STUDY

Robertson, O. Palmer. *The Christ of the Covenants*, pp. 127-146
Vos, Geerhardus. *Biblical Theology: Old and New Testaments*, pp. 66-81

8

Abrahamic Covenant, Part 2

MESSAGE INTRODUCTION

We have begun to see that God's covenant with man is gracious and everlasting, resting on His oath that should it fail, He will be torn in two (Gen. 15). The covenant, of course, by its very nature includes the response of the individual. "Abraham believed, and it was reckoned to him as righteousness" (Gen. 15:6). But never are the works of man the deciding factor in whether or not this covenant gets fulfilled. No, God was fully aware that fallen man could not obey perfectly, so He had (as we have already seen) an eternal plan to send One who would be perfect on their behalf. In this lecture, Dr. R.C. Sproul explores the various elements of the Abrahamic covenant.

SCRIPTURE READING

Genesis 17; 35:1-17

LEARNING OBJECTIVE

To be able to summarize the most important elements of the Abrahamic covenant, and how they relate to Scripture as a whole.

QUOTATION

And God said to him, "Your name is Jacob; no longer shall your name be called Jacob, but Israel shall be your name." So he called his name Israel. And God said to him, "I am God Almighty: be fruitful and multiply. A nation and a company of nations shall come from you, and kings shall come from your own body. The land that I gave to Abraham and Isaac I will give to you, and I will give the land to your offspring after you."

—Genesis 35: 10-12

LECTURE OUTLINE

I. The Abrahamic covenant, cont.
   a. In Genesis 15:8, Abraham asks God the suspenseful question, "How shall I know that I will inherit it" [the land]? God then answers by passing through the animal halves alone.
   b. Just a rudimentary understanding of ancient Near Eastern customs will help us better understand what has taken place in Genesis 15:17. Often in and ANE (ancient Near East), covenants were ratified by the act of cutting (e.g., circumcision, as a sign of the covenant). By passing through the animal halves alone, God is saying that He will experience the curse of the covenant by being ripped in two if He fails to keep it.
   c. The symbols used to describe God as He passed through the gauntlet were a smoking pot and a flaming torch, both reminiscent of the Exodus and the pillars of smoke and fire that led the Israelites (the primary audience of the book of Genesis) through the wilderness. This passing through the animal halves alone gives Abraham the assurance that the covenant will be fully and faithfully kept to the end.
   d. The author of the epistle of the Hebrews hearkens back to this often: 1) It is impossible for God to die; 2) It is impossible for God to lie. God could thus not swear by anything greater than His own name (which He did by passing through the gauntlet alone). Therefore, God's failing the covenant is manifestly impossible.
   e. When Christians struggle with this assurance, we must ultimately look to promises of God through the Christ. When Abraham struggles, he had to look on the promises made by God in Genesis 15.
   f. To be sure, Abraham's participation and obedience were integral to the covenant (cf. 15:6), but in order for the covenant to be everlasting, there must be a covenant-keeper who is Himself eternally faithful.
   g. In like manner, we are saved by the unconditional election of God. That is, God through the Christ met the conditions of the covenant on our behalf. Faith grabs hold of this promise. It is trust in the finished work of Christ. It is not the same as a work of pious obedience, for faith is "the gift of God, not a result of works, so that no one may boast" (Eph. 2:8-9).
   h. The Westminster Confession of Faith, 7.3, sums up this doctrine well. God requires faith in the finished work of Jesus Christ from those who may be saved. It is indeed the condition of the covenant. But that condition rests upon the condition that Jesus already met—that of perfect obedience. God graciously supplies the individual with the ability to meet the condition of faith, or trust, in the redemptive work of Christ on the individual's behalf.
   i. This very same pattern is evident in the Abrahamic covenant.

II. The content of the Abrahamic covenant

a. From Abraham a great nation will come (many in number).
b. His progeny will own the land of Canaan (drinking from wells they did not dig, etc.).
c. Abraham's offspring will be a blessing to all the nations of the world.
d. All of these promises are ultimately brought to pass by the work of *one person*. The rest of Scripture records this story down to that one person.
e. Abraham has a son, Isaac, and the covenant is then passed on to him (Gen. 26). The promise, however, is not given to all of Abraham's children (i.e., Ishmael). Nor is it always passed on to the eldest son. In Isaac's case, Jacob receives the covenant over against Esau.
f. Saint Paul belabors this point in Romans 9. For example, God, of His own free will, and not based on anything Jacob or Esau would or would not do, chose Jacob according to His eternal purpose (9:12-13).
g. The covenant then passes down through Jacob to his twelve sons. Moses uses this to charge the nation of Israel to recognize as their inheritance the land of Canaan, as well as motivate them to faithfully keep the covenant.

III. Circumcision: the sign of the covenant

a. God calls on Abraham to be circumcised as a sign of the covenant between God and Abraham and his progeny (Gen. 17). While Abraham is circumcised after faith in God, Isaac is circumcised before he exhibits faith in God (21:4). Why was this done? Because the promises of God are given to all who believe, but not simply *after* they believe. The promise is a promise whether it is received before or after it is believed.
b. What did circumcision signify? As in other ANE cultures, circumcision was a cleansing ritual. It was understood that infants come into the world unclean. Thus circumcision served as a sign of cleansing, regeneration, purification, and sanctification. But the sign itself (circumcision) and the thing signified (regeneration) are not one and the same.
c. Many Israelites, however, mistook their mere sign of being inside the covenant community as proof of their salvation. In like manner, the sacrament of baptism in the New Covenant has been misunderstood in this way. The sign is a swearing to fidelity and obedience to the God of all grace *after* receiving the benefits of the covenant.
d. This is why we say that sanctification (good works) necessarily flows out of justification. It is not the grounds of our justification. Obedience (sanctification) is to be a response of gratitude to the One who saved us *before* we do any good works (or works of the Law).

STUDY QUESTIONS

1. By passing through the animal halves alone, ___________.
   a. God is saying that Abraham will experience the curse of the covenant by being ripped in two if he fails to keep it.
   b. God is saying that He will experience the curse of the covenant by being ripped in two if He fails to keep it.
   c. God is saying that Isaac will experience the curse of the covenant by being ripped in two if he fails to keep it.
   d. None of the above

2. By which of the following was God represented when He passed through the gauntlet?
   a. A smoking calf
   b. A smoking pot
   c. A smoking torch
   d. Both b and c

3. Since God cannot die or lie, and since He swore by His own name when He passed through the animals halves, then ___________.
   a. Keeping the covenant is manifestly impossible
   b. Failing the covenant is manifestly impossible
   c. Failing the covenant is manifestly possible
   d. None of the above

4. Was Abraham's participation and obedience integral to the covenant?
   a. No
   b. Yes
   c. Sometimes
   d. None of the above

5. Just like the Abrahamic covenant, election unto salvation is ___________.
   a. Conditional
   b. Dependent on man's work
   c. Unconditional
   d. None of the above

6. What did circumcision signify?
   a. Purification
   b. Cleansing
   c. Regeneration
   d. All of the above

BIBLE STUDY AND DISCUSSION QUESTIONS

1. How does the ceremony described in Genesis 15 (and in Jer. 34) relate to other ANE cultures?

2. See B.5 above. What purpose might God have had in setting aside ANE customs as this covenant gets passed down?

3. Does the covenant of grace ultimately rely on human obedience or God's faithfulness to it? Support your answer with Scripture.

4. How is the principle of God's sovereign election confirmed in the story of the patriarch? How does Saint Paul use this story in his letter to the Romans? In what sense does the Apostle speak of election as universal (cf. Gal. 4:22ff.)? In what sense is it individual (cf. Rom. 9:6ff.)?

5. Show from Scripture what it is that circumcision signifies. Show that it is *not* a sacrificial ritual of bodily mutilation (i.e., show that Scripture would prohibit such a thing).

6. Explain how the teachings of Saint Paul (and the rest of the NT) correct the view that one is saved simply by being given the sign of the covenant.

7. Read Leviticus 26:41, Deuteronomy 10:16 and 30:6. What spiritual meaning clearly enjoins itself to the act of circumcision according to these texts? How does this pose a problem for those who would say that the old covenant was purely external in its aim (i.e., that is was not concerned with people's heart-felt responses to God)?

SUGGESTED READING FOR FURTHER STUDY

Robertson, O. Palmer. *The Christ of the Covenants*, pp. 147-166
Vos, Geerhardus. *Biblical Theology: Old and New Testaments*, pp. 81-99

9

Mosaic Covenant, Part 1

MESSAGE INTRODUCTION

By far the most complicated covenant to understand in its relation to the covenant of grace is the Mosaic covenant. This covenant was ratified at Mount Sinai and stands as the definitive marker of the age before Christ Jesus' work on earth. Much confusion abounds about the place of this covenant in redemptive history. In this lecture, Dr. R.C. Sproul seeks to explain the relationship of the Law to the believer (both of the old covenant and new covenant), and discuss the mediating role of Moses in the old covenant.

SCRIPTURE READING

Deuteronomy 5-6

LEARNING OBJECTIVES

1. To understand how Moses served as the old covenant mediator.
2. To be able to list four elements of the Mosaic covenant.

QUOTATION

When I went up the mountain to receive the tablets of stone, the tablets of the covenant that the Lord made with you...written with the finger of God...on them were all the words that the Lord had spoken with you on the mountain out of the midst of the fire on the day of the assembly.

—Deuteronomy 9:9-10

LECTURE OUTLINE

I. The Mosaic covenant
   a. The simple, most basic question we must ask when faced with this covenant in Scripture is, "Is this covenant a reversion back to the covenant of works we saw in the Garden between pre-fall Man and God?"
   b. Romans 3 and 4 tells us that the Law was not meant to be disjoined from the covenant of grace, for the Mosaic Law could never save anyone. The works of the Law are established by the believer who lives in faith (3:27-31).
   c. The Mosaic covenant, then, must be seen as an extension of the covenant of grace. Still, how are we to understand the apostolic contrast between Moses and Jesus, Law and Gospel?

II. Moses the man
   a. Three men in the Old Testament become virtual embodiments of the covenant. They are Abraham, Moses and David.
   b. Moses' place in redemptive history developed over time until he became the key figure in the past age as *the* mediator in God's plan of redemption. The exodus event from Egypt also became the key event that symbolized God's utter faithfulness to His covenant.
   c. Two points in passing are that the revelation of the covenants in Scripture are to be seen as *progressive*. This does not mean that the previous revelation is superseded, it simply means that a subsequent revelation comes alongside the previous one and clears it up, or reveals more fully God's acts.
   d. Another point is that what Jesus is under the New Covenant, Moses was under the Old. He was the prophet (the revealer of God's word).
   e. Moses as mediator: He communicated God's word to the people, and God's word to Abraham was actualized under Moses' leadership.
   f. Under Moses' mediation: 1) The people were gathered together and organized as a nation with their own laws and political structure; 2) The people were brought safely to the borders of the Promised Land; 3) All the people of the world have been blessed as a result of the writing of God's Law; 4) God sustained His presence in the midst of Israel more than in previous times. From the burning bush to the glory cloud over the Tabernacle, God made His presence known.

III. Four elements of the Mosaic covenant (these are not the only elements, but they are essential to understanding this covenant)
   a. The Exodus: Note that the nation's redemption came *before* they were given the Law. This pictures what is always true of God's salvation—it comes by free grace and sovereign choice. The people did not gain God's deliverance by obeying the Law; rather, they watched as God acted on their behalf.

- This event becomes the pivotal event in Israel's history.
- In many ways the Exodus anticipates the redemption found in Christ Jesus. The Christian partakes in an exodus from sin and death into life everlasting.

b. The making of the Mosaic covenant
c. The giving of the Law
d. The ritual of the Law

STUDY QUESTIONS

1. The Mosaic covenant ___________.
   a. Falls under the auspices of the covenant of works
   b. Falls under the auspices of the covenant of grace
   c. Falls under the auspices of the Davidic covenant
   d. None of the above

2. Before the final sacrifice of Jesus Christ, one followed the Mosaic Law ___________.
   a. In order to be saved
   b. In gratitude for God's salvation
   c. To appease the anger of God
   d. None of the above

3. Seeing biblical covenants as "progressive" means that ___________.
   a. The previous covenant is superseded.
   b. All covenants before and after are separated and unrelated
   c. That a subsequent covenant comes alongside the previous one and reveals more fully God's acts.
   d. None of the above

4. Under Moses' mediation ___________.
   a. The Israelites were formed as a nation and entered the Promised Land
   b. All the people of the world are blessed by the writing down of God's Law
   c. God sustained His presence among the Israelites
   d. All of the above

5. Just as in the Exodus event, God's salvation ___________.
   a. Comes before the Law and by free grace and sovereign choice
   b. Comes after the Law and by free grace and sovereign choice
   c. Comes before the Law and by free grace and sovereign foreknowledge of those whom God saw would believe and keep faithful
   d. None of the above

6. Which of the following is not an element of the Mosaic covenant?
   a. The Exodus
   b. The making of the covenant and the giving of the Law
   c. Salvation by works
   d. The ritual of the Law

BIBLE STUDY AND DISCUSSION QUESTIONS

1. In your own words, explain why Moses became such a pre-eminent figure in the history of Israel.

2. Now using Scripture, show how Moses was instrumental in ushering in the great patriarchal promises (at least in their external embodiments).

3. Read Deuteronomy 18:18 and Hosea 12:13. Was Moses merely in a long line of prophets, or was he seen as their head?

4. Read Isaiah 10:26, 11:11, 63:11-12, Jeremiah 23:5-8, and Micah 7:15. Describe the ways in which Moses' work was connected to the great "latter days" when God would re-establish the Israelite kingdom.

5. Read Numbers 12:7 and Hebrews 3:1-6. Can Moses rightly be called the mediator of the old covenant? Why or why not?

6. How did Moses prefigure the Christ with respect to his prophetic role (cf. Deut. 18:15)?

7. How did Moses prefigure the Messiah in his priestly role (cf. Ex. 14:31; 19:9; 24:4-8; 32:30-33)?

SUGGESTED READING FOR FURTHER STUDY

Robertson, O. Palmer. *The Christ of the Covenants*, pp. 167-85
Vos, Geerhardus, *Biblical Theology: Old and New Testaments*, pp. 100-120

10

Mosaic Covenant, Part 2

MESSAGE INTRODUCTION

During the time of Moses, the covenant made with Abraham had begun to see actual fulfillment. Every aspect of the Mosaic law was fulfilled in Christ Jesus, and every aspect pointed to Him. The Mosaic covenant was established *after* Israel's redemption from Egypt. Thus, it was a gracious covenant enacted to draw all the nations of the world to Israel's holy God. In this lecture, Dr. R.C. Sproul continues to expound upon the four major elements of the Mosaic covenant.

SCRIPTURE READING

Exodus 19-20, 24:1-8; Deuteronomy 7-8

LEARNING OBJECTIVE

To be able to summarize the most important elements of the Mosaic covenant, as well as how they relate to Scripture as a whole.

QUOTATIONS

And because you listen to these rules and keep and do them, the Lord you God will keep with you the covenant and the steadfast love that he swore to your fathers....Take care lest your heart be deceived, and you turn aside and serve other gods and worship them; then the anger of the Lord will be kindled against you, and he will shut up the heavens, so that there will be no rain, and the land will yield no fruit, and you will perish quickly off the good land that the Lord is giving you....It is not with you alone that I am making this sworn covenant, but with whomever is standing here with us today before the Lord our God, and with whomever is not here with us today.

—Deuteronomy 7:12; 11:16-17; 29:14-15

LECTURE OUTLINE

I. First element of the Mosaic covenant: the Exodus
   - See previous lecture

II. Second element of the Mosaic covenant: the making of the Mosaic covenant
   a. The people swear allegiance to the covenant-maker (Ex. 24:1-8). Note that this is not an agreement between two equal parties. It is more like a pact made between a king and a vassal.
   b. At Mount Sinai, God recounts what He had done for them (Ex. 19:4). He then charges them to become sanctified (v.9). Before the conditions of the covenant are given, the people must be made clean.
   c. Two further points can be gleaned from this event: 1) Expiation (the remission of sins): Wickedness must be removed from the camp at Sinai before God could reveal His Law (and by extension, Himself) to the people; 2) The Ten Commandments are given in the midst of a national covenant. The commandments themselves are not conditions that if met, will result in deliverance. No, God had already done that. Living out the Law meant living a life of gratitude to God, as well as a means to draw all the surrounding nations to the one true God.

III. Third element of the Mosaic covenant: the giving of the Law
   a. The giving of the Law was to set up a theocracy in Israel. That is, God was to be their king. This is the covenantal aspect of the Decalogue that most resembles other ANE treaties.
   b. In these ancient cultures, suzerains (kings) would make treaties with their vassals. This was very popular in the Hittite kingdom. The 20th chapter of Exodus does share some similarities in its structure with these other non-biblical treaties. They are as follows:
      - Preamble (20:2a): "I am the Lord your God...." The suzerain would identify himself and his stature to the people.
      - Prologue (v.2b): "...who brought you out of the land of Egypt, out of the house of bondage." The suzerain would then rehearse his shared history with the people, and how he has taken care of them.
      - Stipulations (vv.3-17): "You shall have no other gods before me...." The suzerain then spelled out the blessings that would come upon those who obeyed him and the curses that would befall those who disobeyed him.
      - Public reading (24:7): The suzerain then confronted the people by reminding them of their obligations to him, and to update their shared history (as time went on). It also was a means to renew vows. We can see this happening throughout the Old Testament Scriptures.

c. We must also remember that keeping the Law was not salvific, for God had already delivered them. Obeying Him does not *earn* His favor, grace, or choice; rather, obeying sustains the covenant. That is, obedience keeps the people in covenant with God.

d. In the New Testament we see that the Law is not a means for justification but for sanctification ("If you love me, you will keep my commandments," John 14:15). Saint Paul speaks of the Law as a tutor, or schoolmaster, who reveals to us our need for the Gospel.

IV. Fourth element of the Mosaic covenant: the ritual of the Law

a. In all the liturgy of the Mosaic covenant, we see a glorious anticipation of the New Covenant.

b. Two terms are important for us to learn with respect to the foreshadowing of the Mosaic Law:
   - Symbol: A symbol represents something beyond itself that is a present reality. For example, the tabernacle symbolized the presence of God. The tent itself was not *the* presence of God, but it pointed to His nearness to His people.
   - Type: A type refers to something in the future, which reaches a greater, or fuller, fulfillment in the thing to which the type refers (called an "antitype"). For example, the tabernacle is a type of the antitype Jesus. Saint John wrote in his prologue to the gospel that Jesus dwelt ("tabernacled") among us (1:14). In other words, the Incarnation fulfilled in a greater way what the Old Testament tabernacle signified.

c. We see this type/antitype dialogue most often in the Hebrews. This is also why the Church does not practice the OT rituals, because they ended in redemptive history through the coming of the Messiah (since He fulfilled them all). No aspect of the Mosaic covenant is antithetical to the Gospel (as some argue); rather, it prefigured and pointed to the Gospel.

STUDY QUESTIONS

1. The making of the Mosaic covenant is like a pact ___________.
   a. Made between kings
   b. Made between a king and vassal
   c. Between two equal parties
   d. None of the above

2. At Mount Sinai, God recounts how He saved Israel; He then charges them to be sanctified. What does this convey?
   a. Expiation and the obedience to the Law in gratitude, not for salvation
   b. That before the people may be set apart, purified, or made clean, they must be given the conditions of the covenant

   c. That before the conditions of the covenant are given, the people must be set apart, purified, or made clean
   d. Both a and c

3. Theocracy means ___________.
   a. That a small group of holy people rule the nation
   b. That God is king, and that His laws are to be enforced in the land
   c. That God and a chosen king are equal rulers
   d. None of the above

4. The covenantal aspect of the Decalogue resembles which of the following?
   a. It does not resemble anything in the ancient world.
   b. Arabian sheikh treaties
   c. Persian satrap treaties
   d. Hittite suzerain treaties

5. Which of the following is not an aspect of the giving of the Law?
   a. Preamble and Prologue
   b. Bloodletting and Idol Worship
   c. Stipulations and Public Reading
   d. None of the above

6. Two major aspects of the ritual of the Law are ___________.
   a. Prophecy and dancing
   b. Eating raw meat and carving statues
   c. Symbol and type
   d. All of the above

BIBLE STUDY AND DISCUSSION QUESTIONS

1. Search the Old Testament for the numerous references to the Exodus event that describe it as *the* Old Testament redemption. How does this challenge the common opinion of many Christians that the Old Testament is irrelevant?

2. How are the themes of deliverance from bondage and sin, God's display of power and sovereign grace, and the Passover in the exodus from Egypt defining features of salvation as portrayed in *both* the Old and the New Testaments?

3. Read Exodus 19 and 24. In the making of the covenant between God and Israel, what was the great emphasis according to these texts (cf. 19:5, 8: 24:3)? Are the Israelites seen parleying with God about the nature and content of the covenant? Why not? What, then, was required of the people?

4. Re-read Exodus 24:9-11, then 24:3-8. Now read Exodus 12:1-11. How do these events resemble the Passover, and how does it relate to biblical covenants?

5. The giving of the Law, as mentioned in the lecture, served in one sense to organize the nation as a theocracy. What was this theocracy to have looked like? What was it supposed to typify (point to, embody, anticipate)?

6. As pointed out in the lecture, the Law had been given *after* the redemption from Egypt had been accomplished, and the Israelites had already begun enjoying many of the blessings of the covenant. What, then, was the Law for? From our standpoint in the new covenant, what is the Law for? Have the purposes changed?

7. The ritual law is said to have prefigured the Messiah in many ways. Describe in your own words as many ways as you know of that the ceremonies of old typified the coming Christ. Include in your discussion the following: symbol and type, the tabernacle, and the sacrificial offerings.

SUGGESTED READING FOR FURTHER STUDY

Robertson, O. Palmer. *The Christ of the Covenants*, pp. 185-99
Vos, Geerhardus. *Biblical Theology: Old and New Testaments*, pp. 121-74

11

Davidic Covenant

MESSAGE INTRODUCTION

As biblical history continued to unfold, so, too, did God's revelation through covenants. To be sure, it gets more complex, but also much more full when revealing God's glory. In this lecture, Dr. R.C. Sproul discusses the Davidic Covenant—its patriarchal roots, its promises, and its Messianic themes.

SCRIPTURE READING

2 Samuel 7; 2 Chronicles 6:12-42

LEARNING OBJECTIVE

To be able to summarize the most important elements of the Davidic covenant, and how they relate to Scripture as a whole.

QUOTATIONS

"Thus says the Lord of hosts, "I took you from the pasture, from following the sheep, that you should be prince over my people Israel... And I will make for you a great name, like the name of the great ones of the earth... And I will give you rest from all your enemies. Moreover, the Lord declares to you that the Lord will make you a house. When your days are fulfilled and you lie down with your fathers, I will raise up your offspring after you, who shall come from your body, and I will establish his kingdom. He shall build a house for my name, and I will establish the throne of his kingdom forever... When he commits iniquity, I will discipline him..., but my steadfast love will not depart from him... And your house and your kingdom shall be made sure forever before me. Your throne shall be established forever.

—2 Samuel 7:8-9, 11-16

LECTURE OUTLINE

I. Patriarchal roots of the Davidic covenant
   a. In Jacob's prophetic blessing of his twelve sons in Genesis 49, we see the patriarch pass over Reuben, Simon, and Levi and give Judah the ultimate blessing.
   b. He calls Judah (whose name means "praised"; cf. 29:35) a "lion's cub" (v.9). Note that the phrase "lion from the tribe of Judah" finds its origins here.
   c. In verse ten, Jacob says that "the scepter shall not depart from Judah," which signifies that royalty will come from this tribe (cf. 2 Sam. 7:16). This dynasty shall not depart, Jacob adds, "until tribute comes to him." Other versions of the Bible render this phrase, "until he comes to whom it belongs," "until Shiloh comes," and "until he comes to Shiloh." Whatever the absolute meaning, all interpretations see this phrase as referring to the Davidic covenant, and quite possibly to the coming of the King greater than David.

II. God's covenant with David: 2 Samuel 7
   a. David, a skilled military leader and diplomat, sought to unite the people of Israel by moving the capital city from Shiloh (located in the heart of the northern kingdom) to a more neutral location—Jerusalem. David intended to build God a sanctuary, and God's prophet, Nathan, gave his blessing.
   b. But God called on Nathan to speak His word to the king and declare the terms of the covenant:
      - Regarding David's initial desire to build a sanctuary for the Lord, God responds in the negative. On the contrary, He will build David a house—not one made of cedar, but a dynasty. David's royal line did last a long time in comparison to other dynasties in history (400 years compared to the northern kingdom's 100 years, and Egypt's 250 years).
      - A spiritual aspect was also added to the political establishment of the Davidic throne: the kings would serve mediatorial roles in the theocracy as "sons of God." This pointed beyond itself to the perpetual kingdom of the Lion of Judah Himself.

III. Sonship
   a. In Psalm 2, a "messianic" psalm, the king cries out against the rulers of the world who have gathered together to plot against the Lord and His anointed (in Greek, the word is Christos).
   b. He also writes that the Lord has set His king on the holy hill of Zion (v. 6). While this has primary reference to the Davidic king, it has a greater application to the Christ, the King of kings.

c. In 2 Samuel 7:14-16 we see the sin of Solomon referenced (cf. 1 Kings 11:1ff.). As a result of Solomon's turning away, God tore the kingdom from him, but not in his lifetime, "for the sake of David [his] father" (1 Kings 11:12).
d. In the end, David's throne did indeed fall. What, then, of God's promise? The prophet Amos addressed this directly: "In that day I will raise up the booth of David that is fallen and repair its breaches, and raise up its ruins and rebuild it as in the days of old..." (9:11).
e. From this restoration onward, the Davidic throne will endure forever. Thus, we see once again that the predictions and psalms of old pointed through their original meanings to the coming Messiah who would reestablish God's kingdom on earth.

STUDY QUESTIONS

1. In what book and chapter of the Bible does Jacob bless his twelve sons?
   a. 2 Samuel 7
   b. Genesis 49
   c. Deuteronomy 33
   d. Genesis 27

2. What does he predict about the line of Judah?
   a. That royalty shall come from his older brother's tribe
   b. That royalty shall come from his tribe
   c. That the priesthood shall come from his tribe
   d. That a great prophet shall come from his tribe

3. To which of David's offers did God respond in the negative?
   a. His offer to move the ark to Shiloh
   b. His offer to build the temple in Jerusalem
   c. His offer to provide the Northern tribes security
   d. His offer to build a synagogue in Jerusalem

4. What was God's counter-offer?
   a. God would build the temple Himself
   b. God would repeal His covenant with Moses
   c. God would make a dynasty out of David's family
   d. None of the above

5. Which king was greater than David?
   a. Solomon
   b. Jehosophat
   c. Asa
   d. Jesus

6. At the time of the restoration of the Davidic throne, the prophets declared ____________.
   a. That David would be reincarnated and rule once again
   b. That its longevity depended on the people's response
   c. That the reestablishment would last until the Messiah came
   d. That it would never end

BIBLE STUDY AND DISCUSSION QUESTIONS

1. While the word for covenant (*berit*) is not used in the portion of Scripture that describes God's dealings with David, how do the following passages describe this event? How do these passages serve to bind the Davidic covenant to the other covenants of God's progressing revelation? 2 Samuel 23:5; Psalm 89:3; 132:11-12

2. Read 2 Samuel 5:6-7 (and B.1 above); 6:1-2, 7b; 7:1. What three events are described here? How were they used in God's providence to prepare the way for His covenant with David? With an eye on eschatology, how did this scenario anticipate the last days, the kingdom of peace?

3. Read 2 Samuel 7:5 and 11. Describe the situation, and how God plays on the word "house." What is God promising David? Read 2 Samuel 5:3. How does being a king in this theocracy parallel the prophet and priest roles in covenant mediating?

4. Read 2 Samuel 7:14. How is the relationship between the earthly king and the heavenly king described? Why is this significant? (cf. Ps. 2:7; Isaiah 9:6; Rom. 1:3-4; Heb. 1:5).

5. Did the Davidic covenant flow out of the Mosaic or Abrahamic covenant? Does it have to be "either/or"? Why or why not? Include in the answer your understanding of biblical revelation and how it unfolds (progressively or otherwise).

6. Read 1 Kings 2:1-4; 9:4-5. Did David see this covenant God had made with him as a supplanting covenant over the one established at Mount Sinai?

7. The biblical history of the Israelite nation from the time of the Davidic covenant onward is not pretty. Through apostasy, the nation is finally exiled from the Promised Land. But read 2 Kings 25:27-30 and 2 Chronicles 36:22-23. Why, in the midst of covenant cruses, is there this glimmer of hope? How, then, does the Davidic covenant parallel themes from both the Abrahamic and the Mosaic covenants?

SUGGESTED READING FOR FURTHER STUDY

Robertson, O. Palmer. *The Christ of the Covenants*, pp. 229-269

12

The New Covenant

MESSAGE INTRODUCTION

In this the first of three lectures on the new covenant, we will look at the summing up of all the old covenant in the work of one man—John the Baptist. How are we to understand his baptism? How does his work as the fore-runner of Jesus relate to the theme of biblical covenants? In this lecture, Dr. R.C. Sproul explores the ministry of the Baptizer and his relationship to the new covenant.

SCRIPTURE READING

Jeremiah 31-:27-40; Hebrews 8

LEARNING OBJECTIVE

To understand how the new covenant relates to all the previous covenants portrayed in Scripture.

QUOTATIONS

For when I have brought them into the land flowing with milk and honey, which I swore to give to their fathers, and they have eaten and are full grown fat, they will turn to other gods and serve them, and despise me and break my covenant....Behold, the days are coming, declares the Lord, when I will make a new covenant with the house of Israel and the house of Judah, not like the covenant that I made with their fathers on the day when I took them by the hand to bring them out of the land of Egypt, my covenant that they broke, though I was their husband, declares the Lord.

—Deuteronomy 31:20; Jeremiah 31:31-32

LECTURE OUTLINE

I. The New Covenant
   a. All of the previous covenants pointed beyond themselves to the new covenant of Christ Jesus.
   b. Ezekiel's preaching pointed to the future restoration of the people of God.
   c. Jeremiah 31 spoke of the new covenant as growing out of the old covenant. While there is nothing new about sins being forgiven (v.34), the difference is in degrees. The new covenant, which will bring forgiveness of sins, will bring remission *once and for all.* (cf. Heb. 10).

II. The ministry of John the Baptizer
   a. How are we to understand John's baptism? During the inter-testamental period (lasting approximately 400 years), the baptizing of proselytes (converts to Judaism) became a regular practice.
   b. This is John's baptism. The irony was that John was calling those who were already ethnically part of Israel. By charging them to repent and be baptized, he was saying that despite their ethnic heritage they were still unclean outsiders to the covenant. No wonder his ministry was met with skepticism from the religious elite. By John's time, the kingdom of God was at hand (the axe was laid at the root), so his baptizing also served as an announcement of the restoration of the kingdom through the anointed one.
   c. Jesus taught much the same thing regarding the kingdom: "The kingdom of God is among you," He said to the Pharisees (Luke 17:21). God's kingdom, according to Jesus, had broken into history, and the Davidic throne was beginning to be reestablished—this time for all eternity. The messianic kingdom has come (cf. the "kingdom" parables of Jesus).
   d. But the people generally had a poor understanding of how the kingdom was to take shape. They overemphasized one aspect (the military aspect) at the expense of the others (that their sins needed to be atoned for). This is why at times we see Jesus referring to himself as the "Son of Man" over against the loftier title of "Messiah," for their views of the Messiah were distorted—they had no idea of the suffering He had to undergo. Even the apostle Peter misunderstood this (Mark 8:33).
   e. Moses was a type of Christ since he was the great mediating prophet in the old covenant. But Jesus was both the subject and object of spoken (OT) prophecy. Also, the Aaronic priesthood was superceded by Jesus' priesthood, which is after the order of Melchizedek. Finally, Jesus was the supreme King (cf. Ps. 10). David was also a type of Christ, and he typified Jesus who was the greater, everlasting king.

III. When did the new covenant begin?
   a. Quite possibly, it began in the upper room, when our Lord spoke the words of institution: "This cup that is poured out for you is the new covenant in my blood" (Luke 22:20).
   b. In the above verse, Jesus changed the liturgy of the Passover meal. The blood that was poured out was the blood of the lamb on the doorpost. But in the middle of this supper, Jesus said in effect that His body and blood took the place of the sacrificial lamb—only this time it is perpetually beneficial, that is, the sacrifice was enacted once and for all time.
   c. This new covenant was ratified on the cross. But it did not end there, for Jesus rose from the dead and then ascended, two events that must inform our views of these last days. The ascension was not just a mere "going up"; it was a coronation not of just another Davidic king, but of the King of kings.
   d. Thus, the kingdom of God has already come. To be sure, there are elements that have yet to be fulfilled. This is why during Holy Communion we celebrate not just Jesus' redemptive death, but His ascension (which is to be understood as synonymous with His everlasting session as the victorious king at the right hand of the Father).

STUDY QUESTIONS

1. What is so new about the new covenant?
   a. God became three in one.
   b. The new covenant is for children, too.
   c. Sins are forgiven *once and for all.*
   d. None of the above

2. John's baptism signified ___________.
   a. That the kingdom of God had already come
   b. The inclusion of the outsider into the kingdom of God
   c. That the kingdom of the God was yet a long way off
   d. None of the above

3. Messianic expectations in the first century ___________.
   a. Underemphasized the military role of the Messiah
   b. Virtually ignored the need for a perfect atonement
   c. Were balanced and God-honoring
   d. Overemphasized the fact that the Messiah needed to suffer

4. Why was Jesus a greater prophet than Moses?
   a. He was born in Bethlehem.
   b. He spoke prophetically, and He was Himself the subject of prophecy.
   c. Because He was baptized by John the Baptist
   d. All of the above

5. What took the place of the Old Testament sacrificial lamb?
   a. Each of our own sufferings do.
   b. Jesus' body and blood
   c. Both a and b
   d. None of the above

6. The ascension of Jesus is synonymous with ___________.
   a. His going up to heaven in order to wait to rule.
   b. His coronation as the cosmic King of all creation
   c. His everlasting session as the victorious king at the Father' right hand
   d. Both b and c

BIBLE STUDY AND DISCUSSION QUESTIONS

1. Read Matthew 11:14 and 17:10-13. What does the "if you are willing to accept it" statement by Jesus in 11:14 suggest? Could there have been some people who doubted that John was Elijah?

2. Now read John 1:21. How are we to explain this seeming contradiction? What misconception might John have been challenging in this passage? In what way, then, was John Elijah, and in what way was he not Elijah?

3. Read Matthew 3:2, 12 and Luke 3:9. How does that pivotal phrase, "Repent, for the kingdom of heaven is at hand," relate to John's role as the fore-runner of the Messiah? How does it recapitulate the entire Old Testament (hint: law and prophecy)? Why does he call people to "repent" *before* "the kingdom of heaven" comes? If nothing else, then, what does the coming of this kingdom signify (remember the winnowing fork [Matt. 3:12] and the axe [Luke 3:9])?

4. In general, should the baptism of John (Mark 1:4) and the baptism of Christ (Matt. 28:19; cf. Acts 19:2-6) be separated? Are there any Scripture passages that suggest that those who came from John were baptized again when they came to Christ? So, then, do you think that the disciples of John in Acts 19 were re-baptized (with water)?

5. Read Matthew 3:11, Mark 1:4, and Luke 3:3. What is the expected result of the act of baptism? What was its *purpose*? If baptism actually produces something, can it be a mere symbol? How does this challenge or confirm your opinions about baptism as true conveyor of grace?

6. Still, is the baptism of John and the Christian sacrament one and the same? Why or why not? During the time of the Reformation, two extreme views ruled the day: the Catholics held that John's baptism was a mere sign, a type of that which was to come, while most Protestants held that the two baptisms were not to be distinguished. Is there a middle approach? What, if anything, did John's baptism *not* convey (cf. Matt. 3:11)? What significant event in Church history after the ascension of Jesus conjoins baptism with the Holy Spirit?

7. Read Matthew 3:13-15. What does this passage (esp. v. 14) say about Jesus' character? If the goal of John's baptism was the repentance of sinners/forgiveness of sins, why did Jesus subject Himself to it? Include in your answer how Jesus as *the* Israel identified with the nation through this act.

SUGGESTED READING FOR FURTHER STUDY

Robertson, O. Palmer. *The Christ of the Covenants*, pp. 271-78
Vos, Geerhardus. *Biblical Theology: Old and New Testaments*, pp. 311-329

13

The New Covenant, Part 2

MESSAGE INTRODUCTION

The letter to the Hebrews is a letter that has experienced contortion and abuse at the hands of those who sometimes deviously, sometimes ignorantly, spread wrong beliefs that are not in harmony with other portions of God's Word. It is certainly not a simple letter, though there are doctrines clearly articulated, like, for example, the supremacy of the Messiah over all the types and shadows that preceded Him, or the necessity of faith and repentance in the life of the believer. But then there is all the talk of blood and covenants and apostasy—ideas that have led to much confusion in the Church, mainly through a poor use of interpretive principles. In this lecture, Dr. R.C. Sproul seeks to clearly expound the better promises upon which the new covenant is based.

SCRIPTURE READING

Hebrews 9-10

LEARNING OBJECTIVES

1. To understand why the new covenant is founded on better promises
2. To be able to articulate the importance of the shedding of blood in the covenants of the Bible

QUOTATION

But as it is, Christ has obtained a ministry that is as much more excellent than the old as the covenant he mediates is better, since it is enacted on better promises.

—Hebrews 8:6

LECTURE OUTLINE

I. A new and better covenant
   a. Throughout much of the letter to the Hebrews, the author compares and contrasts the risen Christ and His old covenant counterparts.
   b. In Hebrews 8, the author makes clear that the new covenant is better, because it is enacted on better promises. He also makes mention of the "copy and shadow" of the old covenant rituals that pointed to the Messiah (v. 5).
   c. By way of contrast, the readers are reminded of the ancient, pre-exilic atoning ceremonies of the Israelite nation, and how they were to be observed repeatedly (Heb. 9).
   d. But when the Messiah came, He gave the ultimate sacrifice once and for all. It was perfect in that it was without blemish and fully complete in its efficacy.
   e. To repeat it by continuing to offer sacrifices is to deny this efficacy. Thus, early Jewish Christian ceased observing the ceremonial laws regarding atonement. How could they return to the copies and shadows once the ultimate fulfillment of Christ Jesus' sacrifice had come? (This, by the way, is what the author of the epistle constantly admonishes his readers not to do.)
   f. The key to this comparison is found in 9:11ff. What the new sacrifice of Christ's blood accomplished was infinitely more atoning than the old covenant ceremonies. The contrast takes these two atonements and shows how one is heavenly and infinite while the other was earthly and finite.

II. The attestation of blood: Hebrews 9-10
   a. The remission of sins, from the beginning of the Scriptures onward, always required the shedding of blood. Why? Because in Hebrew culture, *life was in the blood.*
   b. The giving of blood was the giving of life.
   c. Even in the Garden of Eden, Adam agreed to God's stipulations, which would bring death if violated.
   d. In verses 23ff., we see that Christ's sacrifice superseded all previous sacrifices, for better promises required a better sacrifice.
   e. At the turn of chapter 10, the author makes clear that the blood of bulls and goats could not take away sin (v.4). So, what was accomplished during the old covenant atonement ceremonies? Were sins forgiven? Indeed, but on what grounds? Not on the grounds of the blood of the beasts of the field, but on the grounds of Jesus' holy blood.
   f. Thus, the Old Testament saints anticipated the remission of sins that only God could provide. They had faith in His divine providence, and the atoning ceremonies of old pointed to the reality of the cross of Christ. Today, we look back to the cross, and the promises fulfilled therein.
   g. But how is Jesus the *only* mediator between God and man? Because He is the one, true God-Man (Greek, *theanthropos*), the only perfect divine human to

have ever lived. All previous mediators, then, could never enter the heavenlies on our behalf. Thus, the Messiah had to come in the flesh and atone for the sins of His people.

STUDY QUESTIONS

1. The new covenant is better ___________.
   a. Because it is enacted on better ideals
   b. Because it is enacted on better promises
   c. Because it is enacted by a more temperate God
   d. None of the above

2. According to the author of Hebrews, the old covenant rituals ___________.
   a. Were just rituals, signifying nothing in particular
   b. Were dead outward forms of worship
   c. Were copies and shadows that pointed to the Messiah
   d. None of the above

3. The intended audience of the letter to the Hebrews were ___________.
   a. Gentiles scattered abroad
   b. Jewish Christians in danger of returning to the sacrificial system
   c. Jews who were not yet Christians
   d. Gentiles, Greeks, and Romans who were living in Palestine

4. Why is Christ's atoning sacrifice infinite?
   a. Because He lost no blood while on earth
   b. Because He is the infinite Son of God
   c. Because He was killed during the Passover
   d. Because His sacrifice is repeated every time Communion is administered

5. From the very beginning of Scripture, it was taught that the remission of sins required ___________.
   a. Taking religious vows
   b. The shedding of blood
   c. Baptism
   d. None of the above

6. Why did the Messiah have to come as a human?
   a. Because humanity is the essence of perfection

b. To pay off a debt God owed the covenant-breakers
c. To pay off a debt God owed the devil
d. What else could have mediated between God and humanity except the God-Man?

BIBLE STUDY AND DISCUSSION QUESTIONS

1. Describe in your own words the distinction between the covenant of redemption and the covenant of grace. Is making a distinction necessary? Why or why not?

2. In what sense is the new covenant better? Use passages from the letter to the Hebrews to support your answer.

3. In what sense is the covenant of grace essentially the same despite its various headings (e.g., the Noahic, Abrahamic, Mosaic, Davidic, etc.)?

4. Who is the administrator of the new covenant? How does He go about giving its blessings to His people?

5. Read Leviticus 17:11. What kind of atonement does this verse describe (exemplary or substitutionary)? How does this relate to Jesus' death on the cross?

6. If Jesus' death was indeed substitutionary, for what was He substituting? Was it absolutely necessary? Why? Use Scripture to support both answers.

7. Recalling our discussion in lecture one, describe the Messiah's active and passive obedience and how they relate to the life and death of Jesus.

SUGGESTED READING FOR FURTHER STUDY

Robertson, O. Palmer. *The Christ of the Covenants*, pp. 278-300

14

The Christ of the Covenant

MESSAGE INTRODUCTION

Saint Paul made much ado about Jesus being the "second Adam." Jesus lived and died on our behalf in order to secure the blessings of the covenant once and for all. Further, if He was not resurrected then we, as the apostle rightly notes, are the most miserable of people (1 Cor. 15:19). Jesus' going before us in all of the promises actually acts as the guarantee of those promises. In other words, because He was resurrected, we too shall see God in our flesh (Job 19:26). In this lecture, Dr. R.C. Sproul explains how Christ Jesus fully completed the covenant on our behalf, and encourages us to anticipate with hope that final day in which we will be raised to eternal life.

SCRIPTURE READINGS

Romans 5:12-21; 1 Corinthians 15; Hebrews 1

LEARNING OBJECTIVE

To understand the role of second Adam that Jesus fulfilled, and how His work on our behalf opens up the blessings of heaven.

QUOTATIONS

And beginning with Moses and all the Prophets, he interpreted to them in all the Scriptures the things concerning himself....But in fact Christ has been raised from the dead, the firstfruits of those who have fallen asleep. For as by a man came death, by a man has come also the resurrection of the dead. For as in Adam all die, so also in Christ shall all be made alive.

—Luke 24:27; 1 Corinthians 15:20-22

LECTURE OUTLINE

I. The second Adam: 1 Corinthians 15
   a. In the midst of his argument for the resurrection of Christ and the general resurrection of the dead, Saint Paul writes in verse 20: "But in fact Christ has been raised from the dead, the firstfruits of those who have fallen asleep."
   b. Here we see that Christ is called the "firstfruits." By one man came death, so by one man comes the resurrection of the dead; in the first Adam all have died, so in the second Adam all shall be made alive (vv. 21-23). Jesus' work is seen in light of His being the second Adam. He fulfilled or completed what the first Adam failed to do.

II. Justification by works alone?
   a. The answer, which might be startling, is "yes." Jesus was born under the Law. He was tempted in the wilderness, where His probationary period is most clear. Unlike the first Adam, Jesus triumphed.
   b. He was sinless, fulfilling and abiding by every aspect of the Law. He kept God's covenant to the utmost. We can see from this that His sinlessness qualified Him to be a perfect sacrifice, and that He lived an absolutely perfect life.
   c. This perfection is "imputed" to those whom God elected before the foundation of the world. It is "double" in nature: 1) Our sins are imputed to Christ on the cross; and 2) His perfect righteousness is imputed to us. It is an "alien righteousness" (so Luther), someone else's perfection that has come to us from the outside.
   d. We are, therefore, justified by works alone—Christ's works alone. He not only dies for us, but He was raised for us, as well. He was the firstfruits.

III. The Resurrection: 1 Corinthians 15
   a. Because of Christ's sinlessness, it was impossible that the grave could keep Him. He served as the exemplar of our resurrection. He was the first one, and He precedes all those who will be resurrected in faith on that final day.
   b. From his discussion of the resurrection of the dead, Saint Paul moves on to a discussion about the resurrection body in 15:35ff. He points out that there is an analogy in nature that helps us to understand this paradox: a seed's outer husk must die and decay for the life within it to germinate.
   c. Just as every living thing has a body in its own kind, so the natural body differs from the spiritual.
   d. In His conversation with Martha in Bethany; Jesus said that he is "the resurrection and the life" (John 11:25). Not only is Jesus alive, having been raised from the dead, He actually has the power of life within Him. This is so because the second Adam is heavenly, while the first Adam was from the dust and returned to the dust.

e. Thus all those who are in union with Christ Jesus bear His image and are of heaven, even while our natural bodies bear the image of the first Adam and will return to the ground from which they came.
f. In Romans 5:12ff., Saint Paul describes how through the work and victory of Jesus, we are justified once and for all, in good standing even now, awaiting our final glorification.
g. While the covenant with Adam failed because of Adam's willful disobedience, the covenant of grace succeeded and fulfilled the creation covenant through the work of the second Adam. The ultimate in grace is that this work was done in our stead. "In this is love, not that we have loved God but that he loved us and sent his Son to be the propitiation for our sins" (1 John 4:10).

STUDY QUESTIONS

1. In what sense is Jesus called the "firstfruits" in 1 Corinthians 15?
   a. He was the first to die
   b. He was the first among all of His people to be resurrected in the flesh unto eternal life
   c. He was the first among all people to be resurrected
   d. None of the above

2. What does it mean to call Jesus the "Second Adam"?
   a. He was the second man in history to be tempted by Satan.
   b. He was a descendant of the Adamic line.
   c. He was the second Jew to have ever died on a cross.
   d. He fulfilled or completed what the first Adam failed to do.

3. By whose merit are Christians justified?
   a. Their own
   b. Jesus' merit conjoined with their own repentance
   c. Christ's alone
   d. None of the above

4. What part of the old covenant did Jesus keep in His work on earth?
   a. He kept none of it since He established an entirely new covenant.
   b. Every jot and tittle
   c. He kept only the "moral" aspects of the covenant
   d. Both a and c

5. How is Christ's imputation "double"?
   a. Christ's perfection is imputed to every person on earth, and only those who believe have their sins imputed to Christ.

b. The Christian's sins are imputed to Christ on the cross, and Christ's sins are imputed to the Christian.
c. The Christian's sins are imputed to Christ on the cross, and Christ's perfect obedience is imputed to the Christian.
d. None of the above

6. What paradox does Saint Paul pull from nature to describe the final resurrection of believers when Jesus returns?
   a. A seed's outer husk must never die for the life within it to germinate.
   b. A seed's outer husk must almost die for the life within it to germinate.
   c. A seed's outer husk must die and decay for the life within it to germinate.
   d. None of the above

BIBLE STUDY AND DISCUSSION QUESTIONS

1. In what three mediating offices did Jesus accomplish the Christian's redemption? Pinpoint passages that describe Him in each of these roles.

2. Was Jesus mediator as God, or as man (or both)? Why is this important?

3. Who appointed Him to this office, and by whose authority did He act? Support your answer with Scripture.

4. What is meant when it is said that Jesus' being born in the flesh was an act of humiliation? What is meant when Saint Paul writes that He was born under the Law (Gal. 4:4-5), and in what sense did He fulfill or complete it?

5. Search the Scriptures for all the various passages that attest to the fact of Jesus' resurrection, including those portions that predict the event. Why is the validity of this event so important to Saint Paul in 1 Corinthians 15, and why is it important for us today?

6. Whose sins did the blood of Jesus atone for? Support your answer with Scripture.

7. How certain is it that God will be faithful to His promises? What proof (or guarantee) has He given that shows His utter faithfulness? Finally, and in your own words, describe some of the stories of the Bible in terms of the overarching covenantal theme found therein.

SUGGESTED READING FOR FURTHER STUDY

Vos, Geerhardus. *Biblical Theology: Old and New Testaments*, pp. 330-42